CW00548576

and other applicable l[
of this work have ad[
factual material herein
following: unique
coordination, expre[
classification of the information. All rights to this
publication will be vigorously defended.

ISBN 0-7876-4086-7
ISSN 1094-9232

Printed in the United States of America.
10 9 8 7 6 5 4 3 2 1

Sweet Bird of Youth

Tennessee Williams

1959

Introduction

Though Tennessee Williams's *Sweet Bird of Youth* (1959) was his biggest box office success since *Cat on a Hot Tin Roof* (1955), the play came to be regarded as an example of the playwright in decline. It was his second-to-last big success. Even before it opened on March 10, 1959, at the Martin Beck Theatre on Broadway, *Sweet Bird of Youth* had $390,000 in advance sales. The original production closed January 30, 1960, after 375 performances.

Drama for Students, Volume 12

Staff

Editor: Elizabeth Thomason.

Contributing Editors: Anne Marie Hacht, Michael L. LaBlanc, Ira Mark Milne, Jennifer Smith.

Managing Editor: Dwayne D. Hayes.

Research: Victoria B. Cariappa, *Research Manager*. Cheryl Warnock, *Research Specialist*. Tamara Nott, Tracie A. Richardson, *Research Associates*. Nicodemus Ford, Sarah Genik, Timothy Lehnerer, Ron Morelli, *Research Assistants*.

Permissions: Maria Franklin, *Permissions Manager*. Debra J. Freitas, Jacqueline Jones, Julie Juengling, *Permissions Assistants*.

Manufacturing: Mary Beth Trimper, *Manager, Composition and Electronic Prepress*. Evi Seoud, *Assistant Manager, Composition Purchasing and Electronic Prepress*. Stacy Melson, *Buyer*.

Imaging and Multimedia Content Team: Barbara Yarrow, *Manager*. Randy Bassett, *Imaging Supervisor*. Robert Duncan, Dan Newell, *Imaging Specialists*. Pamela A. Reed, *Imaging Coordinator*. Leitha Etheridge-Sims, Mary Grimes, David G. Oblender, *Image Catalogers*. Robyn V. Young, *Project Manager*. Dean Dauphinais, *Senior Image Editor*. Kelly A. Quin, *Image Editor*.

Product Design Team: Kenn Zorn, *Product Design Manager*. Pamela A. E. Galbreath, *Senior Art Director*. Michael Logusz, *Graphic Artist*.

When the play opened, the frank depictions of various corruptions were considered somewhat shocking. Touching on familiar themes for Williams (including lost youth and aging, loneliness, sex, and pretending to be what one is not), *Sweet Bird of Youth* was inspired in part by his own life, though not autobiographical. Williams had written at least eight versions of the play. One version was published in *Esquire* and another, with only two characters (Chance and the Princess), was performed in Miami, Florida, in 1956.

From the earliest Broadway production of *Sweet Bird of Youth,* critics disagreed about the play. While some saw it as another example of Williams's prowess with language and character, others found it disjointed, disorganized, and distasteful. Critical opinion generally declined over time, though scholars were interested in how the play fit in with the rest of Williams's career.

Writing about a 1975 revival of the play, Edwin Wilson of the *Wall Street Journal* wrote

> *Sweet Bird of Youth* is not considered on a par with Mr. Williams's best work, but it has its share of his power and magic both in the characters he has created and in the music of his words. No other writer of the American theater offers the lyricism Mr. Williams does, and it can be heard here. . . .

Author Biography

Williams was born Thomas Lanier Williams on March 26, 1911, in Columbus, Mississippi. He was the son of Cornelius Coffin and Edwina (maiden name, Dakin) Williams. Williams's father, a traveling salesman, was rarely home. The children and their mother lived with her parents in Tennessee until 1918. That year, Cornelius Williams moved the family to St. Louis when he was hired as the sales manager for a shoe company. Though Cornelius Williams was abusive to his family, his son found solace in writing, an interest of his since childhood. By the time he was in high school, Thomas was publishing short stories in national magazines.

After graduating from high school in 1929, Williams entered the University of Missouri at Columbia. He considered becoming a journalist, but was forced to leave school after two years because the Great Depression had limited his funds. Williams went to work for his father's employer, the International Shoe Company, and was miserable. He returned to college for a year at St. Louis's Washington University before being forced to drop out again. Williams finally finished his degree at the University of Iowa in 1938. He dubbed himself Tennessee Williams in 1939, based on a nickname he acquired at Iowa because of his southern accent.

Williams had written plays as early as 1935, some of which were produced locally. He won the Group Theatre prize in 1939 based on a sampling of his plays. This prize led to wider recognition, as well as to a Rockefeller Fellowship in 1940. Williams was able to make his living writing, including a half-year stint as a screenwriter for Metro-Goldwyn-Mayer in 1943. The experience and form did not suit him, and Williams turned to plays fulltime by 1944.

In 1944, Williams had a massive hit with the play *The Glass Menagerie,* which made his career. He won numerous accolades for the work, which had some basis in Williams's own life. Between 1944 and 1972, Williams produced more than a play every two years, many of which were extremely successful. He won the Pulitzer Prize for drama twice. The first to win was what many critics consider his best play, 1947's *A Street Car Named Desire,* followed by *Cat on a Hot Tin Roof* (1955). One of Williams's last big box office hits was 1959's *Sweet Bird of Youth.*

After *Night of the Iguana* (1962), Williams's plays differed in form and content from earlier ones, and many were not critically acclaimed or commercially successful. Many were seen as derivative of his earlier work. Williams suffered a mental collapse in the late 1960s, spending several weeks in a psychiatric hospital. His last minor success was in 1972 with *Small Craft Warnings.* Williams continued to write plays as well as novels and short stories until he choked to death on

February 24, 1983, in his New York hotel suite.

Plot Summary

Act 1, scene 1

Sweet Bird of Youth opens in a hotel room in St. Cloud, Florida. In bed are Princess Kosmonopolis (the alias of aging actress Alexandra del Lago) and Chance Wayne, who has come back to his hometown. While the actress sleeps, Chance drinks coffee. George Scudder appears at the door, wanting to know why Chance has returned. When Chance informs him he wants to see his mother and his girlfriend, Heavenly Finley, Scudder tells Chance that his mother recently died and was buried, and that something has happened to Heavenly. Scudder had tried and failed to contact Chance about these matters. Scudder also warns Chance that he had better leave town before Heavenly's father and brother come after him. Before leaving, Scudder reveals that he will be marrying Heavenly soon.

Chance awakens the Princess. The Princess struggles to remember who he is and where they are. It becomes apparent that Chance is her gigolo. She has been drinking heavily and using hashish, which has contributed to her memory lapse. The Princess talks about being a middle-aged actress who does not want to retire. She has recently made a movie, and when she went to the premiere, she was horrified by herself on screen. The Princess is still on the run from this experience. As her memory returns, the Princess remembers how she became involved with Chance.

The Princess wants to know what Chance wants from her. While she was in her stupor, Chance had her put him under contract with a Hollywood studio of which she owns a part. The Princess tells him that the contract has loopholes and can be invalidated. When the Princess tries to seduce him, Chance pulls out a tape-recording he made of her discussing how she smuggled hashish into the United States. Chance attempts to blackmail her into signing traveler's checks to him. The Princess is offended, but she tells him that if they make love right now, she will give him some money.

Act 1, scene 2

The Princess signs traveler's checks for Chance, but insists that she will go with him to cash them. She is afraid to be left alone. As she puts on makeup, Chance tells her his life story. He was popular here. Instead of going to college, he went to New York and was in the choruses of Broadway shows. Chance also made love to many rich women in New York, giving affection to the lonely. During the Korean War, Chance joined the Navy because the uniform looked good on him. He felt he was wasting his youth, and had a nervous breakdown. After his honorable discharge, he returned home and again become involved with Heavenly. Though they were in love, Heavenly's father, Boss Finley, would not let them marry.

Chance asks the Princess to help him by staging a phony talent contest, which he and Heavenly will win. Chance will then take Heavenly to Hollywood. The Princess does not want the publicity. Instead, she sends him down to cash the checks. Chance wants to show the town he is not washed up, and promises to return with most of the money and the car. The Princess allows him to go, hoping he will come back.

Act 2, scene 1

At Boss Finley's house, Heavenly's father is angry that Chance has returned. He calls in his son, Tom Junior. Finley wants his son to throw Chance out of town because the last time he was here he gave Heavenly a sexually transmitted disease that required her to have a hysterectomy. As they talk, Tom Junior informs him that Chance Wayne has stopped outside and is talking with Aunt Nonnie. Tom Junior calls for Aunt Nonnie, who runs into the house. The Finleys question Nonnie. Though she says she will get Chance to leave town, she also defends him, telling Finley that he was a nice boy before Finley destroyed him.

After Nonnie leaves, Tom Junior becomes upset with his father. Finley is running for re-election with Tom Junior on the ticket. When Finley points out Junior's failings, he strikes back with a reminder that Finley keeps a mistress, Miss Lucy, at the hotel. Tom Junior reports that Miss Lucy has said that Finley is too old to have sex. Finley becomes upset by these words.

Heavenly finally appears. Finley compliments her on her beauty. When Finley tries to suggest how she should behave, Heavenly becomes angry. She reminds him that he drove Chance away and tried to marry her off to a succession of old men. She blames him for Chance's corruption. Finley tries to buy her off with a shopping spree. He also insists that she will be at the televised rally that night at the hotel. When Heavenly refuses to go, he informs her that Chance is back in town, and that if she does not appear, Chance will be harmed.

Act 2, scene 2

At the hotel's cocktail lounge, Miss Lucy tells the bartender that Boss Finley smashed her fingers with a jewelry box for her comments about his sexual performance. The Heckler enters. When Miss Lucy learns of his intentions to bring up Heavenly's unfortunate past, she offers to help The Heckler get into the Finleys' rally.

Chance comes into the bar. Aunt Nonnie soon follows. She informs him that he must leave town. Chance shows her the contract with the Princess's studio and tells her about the talent contest. When Nonnie emphasizes the danger he is in, Chance informs her that life is not worth living without Heavenly.

Chance runs into old acquaintances at the bar.

They do not treat him well, but Chance does not understand what has changed. Miss Lucy enters and talks to him. She knows the truth about Chance's life. One of the old acquaintances tells Chance about the Finley rally that night and what it is about. When the old acquaintances leave, Miss Lucy offers to take Chance to the airport.

The Princess appears, disheveled and incoherent. She chides him for leaving her alone. As Hatcher, the hotel manager, approaches them, Chance insists on taking the Princess upstairs. Boss Finley and Heavenly enter the hotel. Chance and Heavenly come face to face. Before they can say anything, Finley drags Heavenly away.

Though the Princess wants to leave, Chance has to deal with Hatcher and Tom Junior about what happened to Heavenly. Chance demands an explanation from Tom Junior. Tom Junior informs Chance that Chance gave Heavenly a disease and that it will affect the rest of her life. He tells Chance to leave town before midnight or he will be castrated. Chance gets the Princess to go to her room.

Miss Lucy and Chance watch Finley speak on television in the lounge. The Heckler asks his awkward question about Heavenly's operation. Afterwards, he is beaten. Heavenly is horrified by his question, and collapses.

Act 3

In the hotel room, the Princess is on the phone

demanding a driver. Hatcher and his cronies force their way inside, insisting that she leave. She tears into them. Tom Junior enters, demanding to know where Chance is. She says she does not know, and Tom promises to get her a driver. After the men leave, Chance returns. Chance assures her that he is still her driver, though he is in no state to drive.

The Princess tells Chance that she wants him to accept his life with her. Chance calls a Hollywood gossip columnist. The Princess speaks to her and learns that her movie has done very well, which will allow her to make a great comeback. Chance intended for her to tell the columnist about two rising future stars, meaning him and Heavenly, but the Princess does not. The Princess makes plans for her return. As the Princess prepares to leave, she wants Chance to come with her. He will not leave. They both realize how time has affected them. The Princess leaves, and Tom Junior enters with other men to deal with Chance.

Characters

Bud

Bud is a St. Cloud local who used to be friendly with Chance. When Bud and friends see Chance in the hotel cocktail lounge, Bud is rather mean. Like others, he doubts much of what Chance says about himself. At the end of the play, Bud helps Tom Junior with Chance's implied castration.

Charles

Charles is a servant in the Finley household.

Alexandra del Lago

See Princess Kosmonopolis.

Heavenly Finley

Heavenly Finley is the daughter of Boss Finley and sister of Tom Junior. She is also the object of Chance Wayne's obsession. She and Chance were lovers until she contracted a sexually transmitted disease from him. Left unchecked, it led to her having a hysterectomy at a young age. Heavenly still resents the fact that her father would not let her marry Chance before he became corrupted. Despite her problems, Chance still looks at Heavenly as the symbol of his lost youth—one that he desperately wants to recapture but never does.

Tom Finley, Junior

Tom Junior is the son of Boss Finley and brother of Heavenly Finley. Like his father, he is a politician. Tom Junior does not have the power of his father, but has organized the Youth for Boss Finley club. He also acts in his father's interests in other ways. Tom Junior leads the activities to get Chance Wayne out of town. When Boss Finley gives him free reign, Tom Junior intends to castrate Chance as revenge if Chance will not leave town. At the end of the play, it seems likely this event will occur, as Chance refuses to leave.

Boss Tom J. Finley

Boss Finley is a leading political figure in St. Cloud and the father of Tom Junior and Heavenly. Finley is a harsh, domineering man, and he is incensed that Chance has returned to town. Finley would not let Chance and Heavenly marry several years ago, which contributed to Chance's life choices and indirectly led to Heavenly's disease. Though Finley is protective of his daughter, he has also tried to marry her off to many older men. Finley enjoys having power over others.

Fly

Fly is an African-American hotel waiter who

serves coffee and Bromo to Chance at the beginning of Sweet Bird of Youth. Chance promises him a big tip because Fly remembers Chance from happier times. In act 2, scene 2, Fly delivers a message to Chance, who only gives it a cursory glance.

Dan Hatcher

Hatcher is the assistant manager of the Royal Palms Hotel in St. Cloud, Florida, where Princess Kosmonopolis and Chance Wayne are staying and where Boss Finley's political rally is held. Hatcher is the one who informs George Scudder that Chance has checked into the hotel. Hatcher works with the Finley family to get Chance to leave the hotel and the town.

The Heckler

The Heckler is a hillbilly who attends Boss Finley's political rallies and asks questions to expose his hypocrisy. Miss Lucy facilitates his admission into the rally at the Royal Palms Hotel. He asks his question, which concerns the operation that Heavenly Finley underwent. After he asks it, he is beaten up.

Princess Kosmonopolis

Princess Kosmonopolis is the alias of middle-aged actress Alexandra del Lago, a central character of the play. She is ashamed of her life as an aging starlet and embarrassed by her latest work. At the beginning of the play, the Princess does not know who Chance is or where they are.

Media Adaptations

- *Sweet Bird of Youth* was adapted as a film in 1962. This version was directed and written by Richard Brooks. It stars Paul Newman as Chance Wayne, Geraldine Page as Alexandra del Lago, and Ed Begley as Boss Finley.

- Another film version was made in 1987. It was directed by Zeinabu Irene Davis.

- A made-for-television version was filmed in 1989. It stars Mark Harmon as Chance Wayne, Elizabeth Taylor as Alexandra del Lago, and Cheryl Paris as Heavenly

Finley.

The Princess slowly remembers that Chance is her driver/gigolo. She does not want to be left alone but knows that while Chance has been taking care of her, he wants something in return. Chance wants her to get him a studio contract; a means for getting Heavenly out of town; and material symbols of success to show off to the locals. Though the Princess gives him the first and last temporarily, this does not change Chance's destiny.

The Princess tries to help Chance get out of town, but he will not leave. Like Chance, the Princess is afraid of aging and the effects of time, but she is more realistic about her situation than Chance is about his.

Miss Lucy

Miss Lucy is the mistress of Boss Finley. She lives in the hotel in a room paid for by him. Finley's power over her is important to him. When he learns that she has said he is too old to have sex, he hurts her fingers by snapping a jewelry box on them. For this, Miss Lucy takes revenge by enabling The Heckler to get inside the rally. While she wants him to hurt Boss Finley, she is not fully comfortable with The Heckler's implied attack on Heavenly. Miss Lucy is one of the many people who tell Chance that he should not be in town, and she offers to take him to the airport.

Aunt Nonnie

Aunt Nonnie is the sister of Chance Wayne's dead mother, though she now seems to work and/or live with the Finleys. It was she who encouraged and facilitated the previous relationship between Heavenly and Chance, a fact that Boss Finley resents. Nonnie tries to get Chance to leave town. She also begs Boss Finley and Tom Junior not to resort to violence against Chance. It is Nonnie who realizes that Chance's obsessions with Heavenly and with acting are symptoms of a futile desire to return to his pure youthful state.

Scotty

Scotty is a St. Cloud local who used to be friendly with Chance. When Scotty and friends run into Chance in the hotel cocktail lounge, Scotty is rather cold. He doubts much of what Chance says about himself. At the end of the play, Scotty helps Tom Junior with Chance's implied castration.

George Scudder

George Scudder is a doctor in St. Cloud and the chief of staff at the local hospital. He performed the operation on Heavenly after her sexually transmitted disease ran rampant. Scudder also is allegedly Heavenly Finley's future husband. Though Scudder owes much to the Finley family, it is he who comes to Chance at the beginning of the play to learn his intentions and warn him of the trouble he faces. Scudder informs Chance that his mother has died and that Heavenly has had troubles since Chance last saw her. Scudder had tried previously to notify Chance about both matters, but Chance was impossible to track down. When Tom Junior wants Scudder to be part of his plans to take revenge on Chance, Scudder declines because it might jeopardize his career.

Stuff

Stuff is the bartender in the Royal Palms Hotel's cocktail lounge. He has held this job for only a short time, having previously worked as a soda jerk at a drugstore. Though Stuff once admired Chance, he is now a member of the Youth for Boss Finley club. It is he who tells Tom Junior what Miss Lucy says about Boss Finley's inability to have sex. This gets Finley's mistress in trouble and leads to revenge by Finley.

Chance Wayne

Chance Wayne is one of the central characters in the play. He has returned to his hometown of St. Cloud to see his mother and to take his girlfriend, Heavenly, away to Hollywood. Chance has arrived under difficult circumstances. He is now twenty-nine years old, and his primary occupation is gigolo. When Chance originally left St. Cloud, it was to be an actor. While he has had some opportunities, he has been unable to capitalize on them. Chance had better luck making love to rich New York socialites, a life to which he returned after a stint in the Navy and recovery from a breakdown.

Because Chance's lifestyle made it hard to find him, he does not know that his mother has died and that Heavenly has suffered a devastating loss because of a sexually transmitted disease that he gave her on one of his previous visits. Though Chance still loves Heavenly, he is clueless about the effects his actions have had on her and on the town.

Chance has also come to St. Cloud to prove to everyone that he is a success. While Chance is obsessed with recapturing his fading youth, he also has some compassion for the Princess. At the end, Chance will not leave town despite repeated warnings that he will be harmed (castrated) if he remains.

Themes

Sex

Throughout *Sweet Bird of Youth,* the idea of sex and its consequences affects nearly every character's life. Having failed to make it as an actor, Chance's "career" consists of working as a gigolo, selling sex and/or companionship to rich, lonely, often older ladies. He met Princess Kosmonopolis while employed at a Palm Beach resort. Because of Chance's liaisons with many women, he gave his girlfriend, Heavenly Finley, a venereal disease the last time they were together. The innocent Heavenly unknowingly let the disease progress unchecked and eventually had to have a hysterectomy. Sex robbed her of her youth and her ability to have children. Because of this incident, everyone wants Chance to leave town, either for his own safety or to punish him. He does not leave, and it is implied at the end of the play that he will be castrated.

For some characters, sex is related to power and money. Princess Kosmonopolis forces Chance to have sex with her at the end of act 1, scene 1. Because she is in a fog about him during the scene, he tries to take advantage of the situation, demanding that she sign some traveler's checks for him. She only does this after the act is consummated. Along similar lines, Boss Finley keeps a mistress, Miss Lucy, at the hotel. When he learns that she has claimed he is too old to have sex, he takes his revenge. He brings her a diamond clip in a jewelry box, but snaps it closed on her fingers, injuring her, when she opens it. He then leaves her, taking the gift with him. The theme of sex drives much of the action of the play, directly or indirectly.

Time, Youth, and Aging

Many characters in *Sweet Bird of Youth* are obsessed with aging and the ravages of time. Though Chance is twenty-nine years old with thinning hair, he is still handsome enough to attract women like the Princess. Yet the only woman Chance truly wants is Heavenly, who shared a romance with him beginning when she was fifteen years old. Several characters point out to him that she has changed. Because of the sexually transmitted disease Chance gave her, she has had a hysterectomy. Heavenly tells her father at one point, "Scudder's knife cut the youth out of my body, made me an old childless woman. Dry, cold, empty, like an old woman."

But Chance believes that if he can take Heavenly away, nothing will have changed; they will move to Hollywood, and Chance will finally be successful as an actor. Heavenly is a symbol of his youth and his promise that he has lost along the way. When Chance and Heavenly meet face to face, they can say nothing to each other. Still Chance cannot give up on his last vestige of hope and submits to what is implied to be castration at the end of the play.

Princess Kosmonopolis shares Chance's fear of aging. She is really Alexandra del Lago, a middle-aged movie actress who knows that Hollywood favors the young. She does not want to retire, but ran out of the premiere of her latest movie when she saw herself on screen. The Princess is hiding out from her identity, drinking and smoking hashish in hopes of dulling the pain. Chance is a sympathetic distraction, though she is under no illusions about his intentions.

At the end of the play, when Chance tries one last time to get her to help him and Heavenly escape by telling a Hollywood gossip columnist about them as actors, the Princess learns that all is not lost. Her movie is a hit and she is praised as having made a comeback. She never mentions Chance and Heavenly. Though the Princess realizes that her victory over time is only temporary, and that eventually she will be tossed aside by Hollywood because of her age, she relishes her short-term victory. Aging and time are parts of life that cannot be avoided, but only Chance cannot accept that by the end of the play.

Topics for Further Study

- Compare and contrast the character and motivations of Chance Wayne in *Sweet Bird of Youth* with Val Xavier in *Orpheus Descending* (1956). What kinds of pressures are the young men under and how do they handle them?

- Research racial politics in the South in this time period. Was the castration of an innocent African American in the play realistic? Would such a crime have been prosecuted? How has the political situation in the South changed since this time period?

- Compare and contrast *Sweet Bird of Youth* with the film *Sunset Boulevard* (1950). Consider how both the play and the film focus on movie starlets dealing with issues of aging. How do the different artistic forms affect content?

- Research the psychology of people who heckle politicians, entertainers, and other public figures. Why do they heckle? Is heckling an effective means of getting a point across?

Politics and Hypocrisy

While many characters have their hypocritical moments and attitudes, Boss Finley is the biggest example of hypocrisy in the play. Much of this hypocrisy is linked to political ambitions, though some of it is personal as well. An upcoming political election is an important part of the play. Finley is having a televised rally to address voters about the recent brutal castration of an innocent African American. Those who castrated the man wanted to make sure it was known that white women would be protected in Florida. While Boss Finley wants to keep white blood "pure," he condemns the crime in his speech and calls himself a friend to men both black and white.

When The Heckler asks a question related to Boss's hypocrisy, he is beaten. He is the only character who directly challenges the Boss. Chance only does so indirectly. Because Chance will not leave town, he, too, is castrated, with the implicit consent of Boss Finley. Heavenly points out another hypocrisy of her father's. While he married her mother for love, he will not allow his daughter the same privilege. He uses her, and others, to show how powerful he is, though this power is invariably linked to politics and/or hypocrisy.

Style

Setting

Sweet Bird of Youth is a drama set at the time the play was written in the late 1950s. All the action takes place in two settings over the course of one day, an Easter Sunday, in the Gulf Coast city of St. Cloud, Florida. A majority of the action occurs in the Royal Palms Hotel. All of acts 1 and 3 take place in one room in the hotel. The Princess and Chance Wayne occupy this room. Act 2, scene 2 occurs in the cocktail lounge and palm garden of the hotel. The other setting is the home of Boss Finley, specifically the terrace. These settings emphasize a specific time and place—the South during the 1950s, when racial and class tensions were still high. Chance has chosen to return to St. Cloud to reclaim his girlfriend Heavenly and his youth. Yet much of the play takes place in a hotel where he is really not welcome, not where Chance lived as a youth or other places where he might have more fond memories of the past (though he did work in the hotel at one time). This impersonal setting underscores the kind of life Chance now leads and its problems. A hotel is also a central place where the community meets, creating opportunities for Chance to run into people that he used to know.

Special Effects and Images

Throughout *Sweet Bird of Youth,* Williams calls for a cyclorama (a large wall placed at the back of a room or stage) on which to project images onto the stage behind the action. The images are not supposed to be realistic, but are intended to help set the mood of the play and underscore the setting. For most of the play, the image is a grove of palm trees blowing in the wind. The wind goes from soft to loud, depending on the action of the scene. When the wind is loud, it blends with the musical score in a specific sound/song called "The Lament." This is used in act 1, scene 1, for example, when the Princess' memory finally returns and she first mentions that she is in hiding after what she believes has been a disastrous career move. Other images include a daytime image of the calm sea and sky, and a nighttime scene of a palm garden with branches and stars.

A significant use of the cyclorama occurs in act 2, scene 2, during Boss Finley's speech. An effect is created so that Miss Lucy, Chance, Stuff, and others are watching the televised rally in the hotel bar while it is occurring on the same stage. Because the rally takes place in another part of the hotel, Boss Finley, Heavenly, Tom Junior, and the Heckler, among others, walk by the bar and off stage into the ballroom. Those in the bar view the rally by "turning on" the television, which is actually a projection of a big television screen against a fourth wall on the set.

The volume of the television is very loud at first, making it seem as if Boss Finley is yelling.

Stuff, a Finley supporter, is happy with the volume. Miss Lucy complains about the noise and turns the sound down, only to have Stuff turn it up again. When Stuff turns it up, Boss Finley is saying that he does not condone the castration of the innocent black man. Moments later, the Heckler appears on screen. Projecting the television in this matter emphasizes the kind of power Boss Finley thinks he has. He believes he is bigger and louder than anyone else. Because of their tense relationship with Boss, both Miss Lucy and Chance want to turn him down, hearing his message but limiting his impact.

Symbolism

Sweet Bird of Youth is replete with symbolism. All the action takes place on Easter Sunday. The use of this symbolic day of rebirth has been interpreted in several different ways. Boss Finley claims he has been reborn during the rally. On Good Friday, his effigy was burned at a local university, yet he is still alive and in charge on Sunday, preaching on television. By his side is his daughter, Heavenly, who has just been publicly humiliated by the Heckler. The Heckler is severely beaten. But Boss Finley rises above it all. Some critics believe that Chance Wayne has undergone a compacted reversal of the Easter cycle, beginning with Chance's resurrection in the morning and castration (crucifixion) at night.

Another use of symbolism in the play is found in some of the characters' names. Chance Wayne's chances in life are indeed on the wane. Heavenly Finley's first name brings up a number of contradictions. She may still be beautiful, and heavenly to Chance and her father, but she is dead on the inside because her love has been denied and she has had her childbearing abilities taken away at an early age. Though Princess Kosmonopolis is only the alias of the actress Alexandra del Lago, she acts like royalty. She does not accept being condescended to and is always in charge. Kosmonopolis suggests Greek words that mean worldly and city. She is above the petty world of St. Cloud, merely using it for cover as she hides from her real world. These kinds of symbols enrich the text and add some definition to the characters.

Historical Context

In 1959, the United States was on the verge of major transitions, primarily on the home front, though the ever-escalating Cold War between America and the U.S.S.R. was also a constant threat. The country was expanding. Two new states were admitted in 1959: Alaska and Hawaii. Republican President Dwight D. Eisenhower was near the end of his second term. In 1960, Democrat John F. Kennedy would be elected to the presidency, defeating Eisenhower's vice president, Richard M. Nixon.

Many observers believed that Nixon lost at least partly because of his image and attitudes expressed during televised debates with Kennedy. In the 1950s, politicians were televised for the first time. Senator Joseph McCarthy's anti-Communist hearings were televised. Conventions were aired for the first time in 1952. In 1959, the Federal Communications Commission upheld an equal time rule for political candidates. The power of television was soon realized, then exploited, by politicians.

Eisenhower's United States was relatively economically strong in 1959. The country was recovering from a recession in 1957-1958, but generally sound. His government spending bill was scaled down, putting fiscal responsibility before both military and domestic concerns. Credit cards had only recently been introduced; they would have a great effect on the American economy in the coming decades. American Express issued its first credit cards in 1958.

One big issue in the late 1950s was civil rights. The civil rights movement that exploded in the 1960s was based in part on events of the 1950s. In 1954, the Supreme Court handed down a landmark decision in *Brown v. Board of Education*. This case focused on education, addressing the legality of separate schools for whites and blacks. The court ruled that separate was not equal, and that most schools for blacks were far inferior to those attended primarily by whites. Court-ordered desegregation of schools became a public tug-of-war. The actual process of integration was very slow, and many southern states, especially Virginia, fought integration, even as late as 1959 and beyond. True integration was not completed until the 1960s.

In 1959, Eisenhower tried to convince Congress to enact a seven-point civil rights program in a special session. Despite such measures, states like Tennessee continued to hold white primaries in which blacks could not vote. Racism was still rampant in the South. In 1956, Emmett Till was murdered for allegedly whistling at and/or assaulting a white woman. His killers were acquitted, though they were obviously, and later admittedly, guilty. Events like the castration of an innocent African American mentioned in *Sweet Bird of Youth* were not unheard of.

Despite such crimes, moral standards were changing in the United States. In 1959, the Supreme

Court ruled that the postmaster general could not decide what was too obscene to be sent through the mail. The case concerned a book by D. H. Lawrence, *Lady Chatterly's Lover*. While single men were seen as swinging bachelors, women were supposed to be desirable, but untouchable until marriage. Yet the Kinsey Report on sexual activities of Americans in the early 1950s showed that Americans regularly had extramarital sex and that homosexuality was common. Depictions and discussions of sex became more common in movies, novels, and music. Though the government had organized public health officials to diagnose and treat venereal diseases in the post-World War II period, there was a slight rise in rates of syphilis and gonorrhea at the end of the 1950s as complacency set in.

Women's roles were also changing in this time period. More women were working outside of the home, but most were limited to jobs in the service industry or to clerical and assembly line positions. Fewer women attended college than in the 1940s. Only about thirty-five percent of college students were women at the end of the decade, and thirty-seven percent of those left before graduation, most to get married. Career options were limited. There was only one woman in the United States Senate in 1959, Margaret Chase Smith. In the 1960s, women's roles would change and career options would start to expand. By the 1970s, there would be a burgeoning feminist movement. Big changes in American life were on the horizon in 1959.

Compare & Contrast

- **1959:** Political use of television is still in its infancy, though it soon becomes a major force in elections.
  Today: The power of the internet is still limited for politicians, but is expected to become a big factor in the coming years.

- **1959:** There are limited roles for older actresses in Hollywood movies, primarily mother and grandmother-type roles.
  Today: While there is a still an emphasis on youth in Hollywood, there is a greater variety of roles for older women in movies, reflecting the many roles women play in society.

- **1959:** Images of sex and violence are limited in the movies, in part because of a code that restricts such images.
  Today: While there is a movie ratings system in place, there are only tenuous limits on how sex and violence are depicted.

- **1959:** Sexually transmitted diseases are diagnosed and treated in both men and women, though many, especially young women, are not taught how to avoid getting them.

Today: Because of the AIDS epidemic in the 1980s and better sexual education, many young women (and men) are aware of the possibilities of sexually transmitted diseases and know how to avoid getting them.

When *Sweet Bird of Youth* made its debut in 1959, it received a mixed reception. While some critics thought it was another example of Williams's genius, others saw it as lesser Williams. Both sides, however, generally agreed that Williams's command of language had not diminished, and the play was a box office success. Over time, *Sweet Bird of Youth* came to be regarded as an example of Williams on the decline.

Walter Kerr of *New York Herald Tribune* was one critic who praised the play, though like most critics he had some problems with it. He wrote, "There isn't a moment during *Sweet Bird of Youth* that it isn't seething to explode in the theater's face. Mr. Williams's newest play is a succession of fuses, deliberately—and for the most part magnificently—lighted."

Several critics who liked *Sweet Bird of Youth*, and even some who did not, believed that Act 2 did not fit well within the play's structure. For example, Richard Watts, Jr., of the *New York Post* praised the power of Williams's writing but added, "What worried me were a number of loose ends, the lack of complete fulfillment of several characters, and the hinting at themes that were not developed."

Among those critics who praised the play, some were disturbed by the play's content and themes, which were rather shocking for their day.

Brooks Atkinson of the *New York Times* wrote, "It is a play that ranges wide through the lower depths, touching on political violence as well as diseases of mind and body. But it has the spontaneity of an improvisation." John Chapman of the *Daily News* wrote, "I don't see how it can be liked, in the sense that one might like the simple joys of *The Music Man,* but it cannot be ignored. . . ." He added, "Seeing . . . *Sweet Bird of Youth.* . . is something like finding oneself, unexpectedly and without premeditation, in a place one wouldn't be caught dead in."

Other critics were more distressed by the content of *Sweet Bird of Youth.* Marya Mannes of *The Reporter* wrote

> The laughter at the Martin Beck Theatre in New York these nights is made, I think, of. . . a fascination with and amusement in depravity, sickness, and degradation which makes me equally disturbed at the public, the playwright, and those critics who have hailed *Sweet Bird of Youth* as one of Tennessee Williams's 'finest dramas' and 'a play of overwhelming force.'

Along similar lines, Kenneth Tynan of the *New Yorker* argued

> For my part, I recognized nothing but a special, rarefied situation that had been carried to extremes of

cruelty with a total disregard for probability, human relevance, and the laws of dramatic structure. My brain was buzzing with questions. . . . I suspect that *Sweet Bird of Youth* will be of more interest to Mr. Williams's biographers than to lovers of the theatre.

Other critics also dismissed the play as only interesting to those who are fans of Williams. Robert Brustein of *Encounter* argued

the play is interesting primarily if you are interested in its author. As dramatic art, it is disturbingly bad—aimless, dishonest, and crudely melodramatic—in a way that Williams's writing has not been bad since his early play, *Battle of Angels*. But if the latter failed because its author did not sufficiently understand his characters, *Sweet Bird of Youth* suffers both from his ignorance of, and obsession with, himself.

Harold Clurman of *The Nation* concurred. He wrote, "Its place in the author's development and its fascination for the audience strike me as more significant than its value as drama."

Several other critics disliked the play because of dramatic failings. Brustein, writing this time in *Hudson Review,* judged

Williams seems less concerned with dramatic verisimilitude than with communicating some hazy notions about such disparate items as Sex, Youth, Time, Corruption, Purity, Castration, Politics, and The South. As a result, the action of the play is patently untrue, the language is flat and circumlocutory, the form disjointed and rambling, and the characters—possessing little coherence of their own—function only as a thin dressing for these bare thematic bones.

In short, Henry Hewes of *Saturday Review* concluded,"the total play. . . adds up to a good deal less than the sum of its parts."

Sweet Bird of Youth was revived several times over the years, and the critics remained divided, with most having serious problems with the play. Of a 1975 revival at the Brooklyn Academy of Music, Gina Mallet of *Time* wrote

Age has not refined Sweet Bird's effulgent bathos. The reduction of personality to sex organs is the dynamic of skin flicks and soap operas. . . . Today it seems fatally misconceived, a sentimental melodrama instead of a savage, black comedy on southern mores.

A few critics were still impressed by

Williams's creation, including Howard Kissel of *Women's Wear Daily*. He wrote

> In its time, *Sweet Bird of Youth* was a powerful emotional experience; now it impresses one mainly because of the deliciousness of the language. The characters may not be as tragic as they once seemed, but they still have credibility as American archetypes.

What Do I Read Next?

- *Suddenly Last Summer,* a play written by Williams in 1958, shares thematic and dramatic concerns with *Sweet Bird of Youth*.

- *The Little Foxes,* a play written by Lillian Hellman in 1939, concerns rivalries and disloyalties in a southern family.

- *Orpheus Descending,* a play written by Williams in 1956, has themes and characters similar to *Sweet Bird.*

- *Midnight in the Garden of Good and Evil: A Savannah Story,* a novel by John Berendt published in 1994, also concerns sexual mores and eccentrics in the South.

- *The Enemy Time* is a play by Williams published in *Theatre* in March 1959. This one-act play was an early version of *Sweet Bird of Youth.*

Sources

Aston, Frank, *"Bird of Youth* Stormy Drama," in *New York World Telegram and The Sun,* March 11, 1959.

Atkinson, Brooks, "The Theatre: Portrait of Corruption," in *New York Times,* March 11, 1959.

Brustein, Robert, "Sweet Bird of Success," in *Encounter,* June 1959, pp. 59-60.

_____, "Williams's Nebulous Nightmare," in *Hudson Review,* Summer 1959, pp. 255-60.

Chapman, John, "Williams's *Sweet Bird of Youth* Weird, Sordid and Fascinating," in the *Daily News,* March 11, 1959.

Clurman, Harold, Review in *The Nation,* March 28, 1959, pp. 281-83.

Hewes, Henry, "Tennessee's Easter Message," in *Saturday Review,* March 28, 1959, p. 26.

Kerr, Walter, Review in the *New York Herald Tribune,* March 11, 1959.

Kissel, Howard, Review in *Women's Wear Daily,* December 31, 1975.

Mallet, Gina, "Petit Guignol," in *Time,* December 15, 1975.

Mannes, Marya, "Sour Bird, Sweet Raisin," in *The Reporter,* April 16, 1959, pp. 34-5.

Tynan, Kenneth, Review in *New Yorker,* March 21, 1959, pp. 98-100.

Watts, Jr., Richard,"Tennessee Williams Does It Again," in *New York Post,* March 11, 1959.

Williams, Tennessee, *Sweet Bird of Youth,* New Directions, 1959.

Wilson, Edwin, "The Desperate Time When Youth Departs," in the *Wall Street Journal,* December 8, 1975.

Further Reading

Griffin, Alice, *Understanding Tennessee Williams,* University of South Carolina Press, 1995.

> This critical study offers in-depth discussion and analysis of a number of Williams's plays, including *Sweet Bird of Youth.*

Nelson, Benjamin, *Tennessee Williams: The Man and His Work,* Ivan Obolensky, Inc., 1961.

> This critical biography includes a discussion of Williams's plays through the beginning of the 1960s, including *Sweet Bird of Youth.*

Williams, Tennessee, *Memoirs,* Doubleday & Company, Inc., 1975.

> This autobiography encompasses Williams's life and career.

Lightning Source UK Ltd.
Milton Keynes UK
UKHW02f1828191018
330853UK00011B/675/P